Environmental Lifestyle Guide

For Grade 11 Students

VOL.7 OF 11

Do It Yourself (DIY)

Jahangir Asadi

Vancouver, BC CANADA

Published by: Silosa Consulting Group Inc.
Vancouver, BC **CANADA**
Email: Info@Silosa.ca
www.silosa.ca

Ordering Information:
Quantity sales. Special discounts are available on quantity purchases by universities, schools, corporations, associations, and others. For details, contact the "Sales Department" at the above mentioned email address.

Environmental lifestyle Guide Vol.7 for Grade.11/J.Asadi —1st ed.
ISBN: 978-1-990451-81-2

Contents

We hope that, 10,000 years from now, future generations will be able to see flowers that provide bees with nectar and pollen and...
BEES provide flowers with the means to reproduce by spreading pollen from flower to flower,....

Jahangir Asadi

This book is dedicated to my professor, Dr.Bijan Esfandiari

Introduction

This book is part of an eleven volume series that is meant to be a standard textbook series, for grades 9 to 12. TTAIN & ESFK & SCG improves quality of life and reduces environmental degradation by fostering new consumption patterns and sustainable lifestyles through International Cooperative Extension Service programs at houses, offices, schools and libraries all over the globe.

Climate change is real. Therefore people have the potential to make a difference now and for future generations. This book provides climate science basics, including the roles that lifestyles and populations play in the climate scenario, the significance of carbon footprints, and an overview of the current climate situation. The manual has been categorized based on humanity's needs starting first with food and ending with tourism. The manual then illustrates the difference between adaptation (taking steps to live with the changes) and mitigation (taking steps to slow the rate of change.)

Adaptation examples include food, energy, transportation, recreation. Mitigation focuses on effectively engaging with local governments, through serving on advisory boards, communicating with public officials, educational institutes, schools, universities, libraries and leading communities towards climate change actions.

One useful way to mitigate climate change is through increasing public knowledge to better understand the impact of the rate of change on plants and animals. This is crucial for preserving species; and for assessing potential insects and disease outbreaks in agriculture, natural resources and public health.

Taking personal action is a key element of this manual.

Citizens are challenged to consume 20% fewer resources, to bring world consumption levels down as much as possible. Readers are given 12 practical steps to take to make the changes. The resources section provides additional information, and readers are encouraged to contact the author for further questions.

As an accessibility action, we have provided Online international courses on climate change control as well. You can access the courses via the following link:

http://TopTenAward.org

SILOSA Consulting Group (SCG)

Silosa Consulting Group (SCG) was established to provide outstanding consulting services of management system & educational standards to individuals, groups, companies, schools, and organizations all over the globe. SCG is publishing an "Environmental Lifestyle Guide " book series as a standard textbook related to increasing environmental awareness of students means being aware of the natural environment and making choices that benefit the earth, rather than hurt it. Vol.1 to 11 (for grades 9 to 12) providing some of the ways to practice environmental awareness include: **Recycling**, **Conserving energy and water**, **Reuse, Activism, and others**.

SCG book publishing services and distribution services are connected to over 39,000 booksellers worldwide, including Apple, Amazon, Barnes & Noble, Indigo, Google Play Books, and many more. SCG has enough experiences to help create new and effective environmental educational programmes in different countries all over the world. For more detail, visit our website : http://silosa.ca and/or send your enquirer to the following email:

info@silosa.ca

CHAPTER **1**

About ISO 14000 for Students

The International Organization for Standardization is an independent, non-governmental organization, the members of which are the standards organizations of the 165 member countries. It is the world's largest developer of voluntary international standards and it facilitates world trade by providing common standards among nations. More than twenty thousand standards have been set, covering everything from manufactured products and technology to food safety, agriculture, and healthcare.

Kids ISO 14000s
"Kids ISO 14000s" is a new environmental education program for children, based on ISO 14000s, which is international standard for environmental management. Primary aims of this program are: -
1. To teach and train children how to manage the environmental issues (such as energy saving) by themselves through the working book and guide book of this program,
2. To certify those children who showed good accomplishment in the program from highly international authority (as is the case of ISO 14000s)
3. To network those children through the international network (Kids International Network), so that the children can work on the environment, internationally.

2. System of Kids ISO 14000s Program

The system of Kids ISO 14000s Program consists of

1. Operation Headquarter (ArTech).

2. Workbook, Guidebook (originally published by ArTech, and local versions are produced by each countries).

3. Eco-Kids-Instructors for local operation and evaluation of the performance of the children.

4. International accreditation committee for accreditation of accomplishment of the children, for certification of the Eco-Kids-Instructors, as well as overall checks of this program.

5. Linkage with international organizations (such as UNU, UNESCO, etc. …) And also national organizations

More information can be obtained :

www.ISO.org

Canada

Environmental Sustain for Future kids established in Vancouver, BC Canada in 2020. (ESFK) is an international ecolabel focused on taking care of environment for future of kids. ESFK defined as 'self-declared' environmental claims made by manufacturers and businesses based on ISO 14020 series of standards, the claimant can declare the environmental objectives and targets in relation to taking care of environment for future kids. However, this declaration will be verifiable.

Environmental Sustain for Future Kids
Vancouver, BC CANADA

Email: info@esfk.org
Web: www.esfk.org

All about 'Eco-friendly'
DIY Building, Modifying, and/or Reconstruction

D IY is short for do-it-yourself. It means carrying out home repairs, maintenance, and improvements yourself instead of hiring a professional. Interest in DIY took off after the Second World War. Changes such as growth in home ownership and the arrival of TV programs about home improvement helped to fuel the DIY movement.

After a while our homes need a change or some updating. They can seem tired and old and in need of a little refreshing. Ideally, perhaps, you might like to move to a larger home but the economy has you worried and you want to spend your money wisely. So instead, you've decided to renovate your home not only to perk it up but to better accommodate your current needs and lifestyle. If you haven't thought to do so already, you might want to think about some environmentally savvy ways to renovate your home.

Top Ten Eco-Friendly Ways to Renovate Your Home

If you are planning on renovating your home, you'll want to make sure you do it in style but without further causing harm to our environment. Contrary to what many people think, there are plenty of ways to make your home renovation an environment-friendly one. That way, you have a home that is not only aesthetically pleasing, but one that reduces environmental impact. But how exactly do you renovate a home to make it simultaneously eco-friendly and stylish? we show you Top Ten of eco-friendly ways to renovate your home:

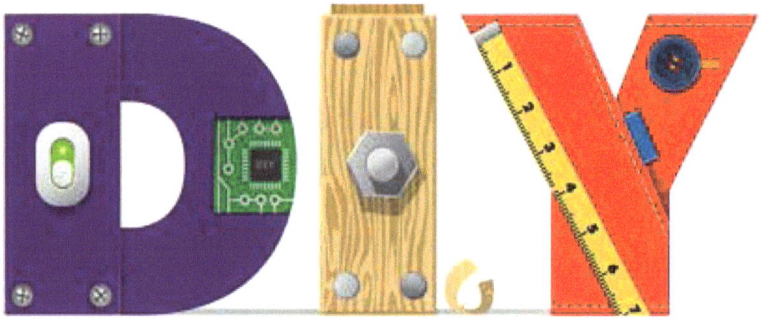

1. Use recycled glass

There are many home depots that now cell bio-glass that look like new windows but are 100% environment-friendly. They make a fantastic addition to the kitchen or your bedroom, as it brightens the whole space allowing natural lighting and morning sunshine – a great way to start your morning!

2. Use formaldehyde-free cabinets

Formaldehyde is commonly used in building materials and household products. But even if it's found in many household and beauty products, it's actually quite toxic! We recommend that you look for those free of this arterial to ensure safety for both your home and the environment's well-being. There are now many stores that offer VOC and formaldehyde-free furniture such as kitchen cabinets.

3. Paint with low-VOC or VOC-free paint

VOC is short for volatile organic compounds which produce harmful molecules. This ends up with you and the household incurring long-term health effects, and they aren't good ones either! Using VOC-free products like paint will help you breathe easier when at home.

4. Go solar

The sun is very powerful and it's a renewable source of energy – so use it to your advantage! Collecting the power of the sun via solar panels can give you electricity to last the whole night and you can use it to heart's content completely guilt-free! Not only will you help the environment through saving energy, but you will notice your electricity bills becoming less expensive as well. (For complete detail in this regard refer to IEL Vol.2 Energy)

5. Deconstruct your home – don't demolish it!

If you plan on tearing down walls or even knocking down entire rooms, walk around your home first to see what you can salvage and re-use beforehand. Not only is this eco-friendly, but it will save money in the end. If it ain't broke, don't fix it! Most likely there is a ton of material you can salvage and re-use. Consider everything from light fixtures, to flooring, tile, bricks, cabinets and molding. If you plan on replacing the chandelier in your dining room, instead of tossing it, think about using it in another room – maybe your kitchen, your daughter's bedroom, even a bathroom!

6. Choose bamboo flooring

What makes bamboo different from other types of wood materials? It's durable, moisture-resistant, grows back faster than wood and growing it uses less pesticides. We have an abundance of bamboo that can be harvested without destroying its roots, making it an environmentally friendly option. You get to save the lives of other trees and old growth forests, all while getting sleek chic flooring. Just make sure to get a good hammer to carry out this project; plus, it's energy-saving as well!

7. Using salvaged wood or discarded metal & Donate your unwanted items

Using recycled materials such as wood and metal will help to reduce waste and the need for fossil fuels as trucks and machinery aren't required to cut down existing trees. Plus, it gives your home a unique and contemporary look. Don't worry about rust or damage, as there are many types of salvaged materials that hold durability and beauty. So you really don't want that dining room chandelier in any other room. So you really don't want that dining room chandelier in any other room. Don't toss it, Perhaps you even have a crafty friend who might enjoy repainting and re-purposing it. With this in mind, not only are you being environmentally friendly, but you are truly giving back to the community.

8. Focus on energy-efficient appliances

If you're planning to replace refrigerators, air conditioners, or other types of major appliances, focus on those that help save both the environment and energy. Investing in energy efficient white goods will go a long way to saving you money in the longer term! (For complete detail in this regard refer to IEL Vol.2 Energy)

9. Consider buying pre-owned materials

Habitat for Humanity is one such retailer, but there are many across the country, some even specialize in high-end products. This can be a great and cost-effective way to redo your home. If, in the end, that SubZero fridge is an absolute must have, you could save thousands of dollars buying one that has been used for a couple of years. Cabinets may be the largest expense of a kitchen renovation, these salvage shops often have high quality cabinets in fabulous condition. It's an idea certainly worth investigating.

10. Re-face instead of replace

As I just mentioned, the greatest expense of any kitchen remodel may very well be your cabinets. Instead of replacing them altogether, consider repainting them or simply refacing them. Most likely your cabinets are in great conditions. New doors and drawers can give seemingly tired cabinets a whole new life!

Conclusion:

Looking for a way to renovate your home while saving the environment isn't all that difficult if you follow these eco-friendly renovation tips. And these helpful hints don't just apply to your home – they can apply to your office, work space or any other building project you're thinking of undertaking!

Do you have any other tips or suggestions on how to renovate your home in a more sustainable way? Please let us know for considering in the next edition of this International Environmental Volume Series.

Most Popular Eco-Friendly Flooring Solutions

We have provided a guide of the most popular eco-flooring solutions, some are new, some are old and a few will make you think:

1. Cork

Cork flooring is a product made from the bark of the cork oak tree, a material which is ground, processed into sheets and baked in a kiln to produce tiles that serve as flooring for offices, light commercial locations, and residences. Cork is harvested from the bark of the cork oak tree commonly found in the forests of the Mediterranean. The trees are not cut down to harvest the bark, which will grow back every three years, making it an ideal renewable source. It has anti-microbial properties that reduce allergens in the home, is fire retardant, easy to maintain and acts as a natural insect repellent too.

2- Bamboo

Bamboo flooring is another wood like option that is gaining in popularity. It is actually a grass that shares similar characteristics as hardwood. It is durable, easy to maintain and is easy to install. Bamboo is sustainable and made from natural vegetation that grows to maturity in three to five years, far less than the twenty years trees can take.

Bamboo, while usually very light, is available in many hues that will work in any setting or decor. Its varied grains and wide array of colors give it an edge over traditional flooring by allowing for customization not often found elsewhere.

FLOOR AND MATERIAL ICONS

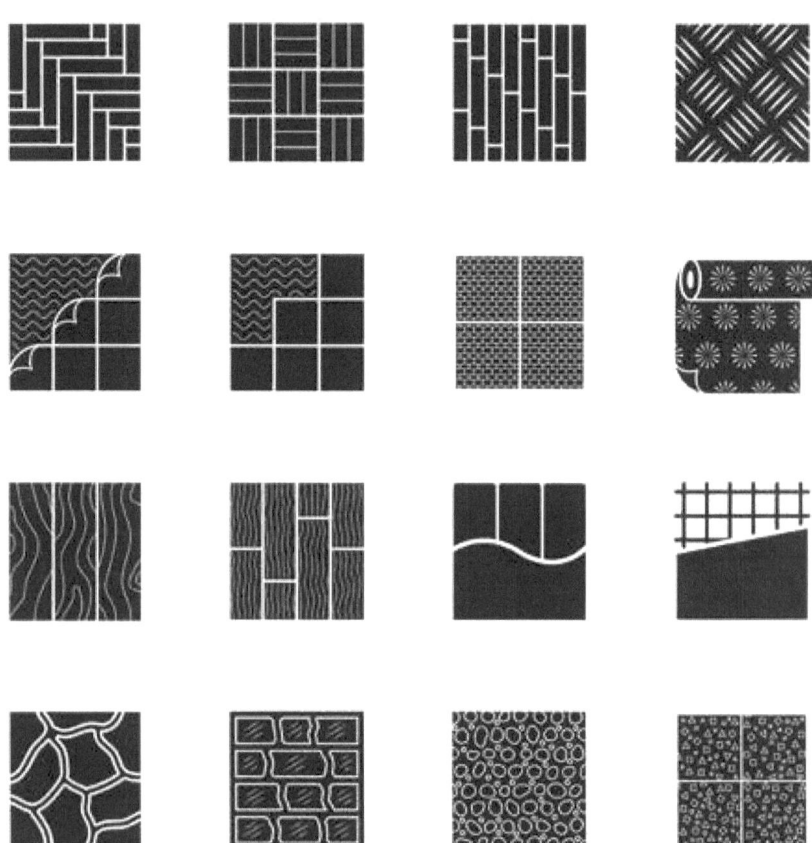

3. Linoleum

Linoleum is one of the most natural and sustainable flooring solutions on the market, appreciated for its natural beauty, comfort and durability for over 150 years. When one thinks of linoleum flooring, vinyl tends to come to mind and yet the two are nowhere close to each other. Vinyl is a synthetic made of chlorinated petrochemicals that are harmful. Linoleum is created from a concoction of linseed oil, cork dust, tree resins, wood flour, pigments and ground limestone.

Like cork, it is fire retardant and water resistant. Linoleum is not new to the market; it fell out of favor with the introduction of vinyl in the 1940's. As architects and designers began asking for it again, it reemerged with a vast array of bright vibrant colors and a new sealer to protect it from stains. It has a long shelf life and will hold up to a lot of wear and tear. In addition to being made with renewable materials, linoleum is biodegradable and won't take up space in landfills. Linoleum does not emit harmful VOCs (brand new linoleum does have a harmless odor from the linseed oil content that dissipates after a few weeks).

4. Glass tiles

Ever wonder what happens to the beverage bottles that are shipped to the recycler? They are converted into beautiful glass tiles. This renewable source is fast becoming a wonderful option for floors as well as bathroom and kitchen walls. Glass has similar benefits of other eco-friendly materials. It is non-absorptive and won't mildew or mold in damp environments. It is easy to maintain and won't stain.

Glass comes in a limitless array of colors, patterns and finishes suitable for most design schemes. Unlike ceramic tiles, glass will reflect light rather than absorb it, adding that additional layer of light some rooms need.

5. Concrete

Polished concrete is an unlikely sustainable material that is gaining in popularity. Concrete is typically slab on grade and used as a sub flooring in some residential settings. If it is polished and tinted to the homeowners taste and style there is no need for traditional flooring to be put over it.

From creating a tiled effect with different colors to inlaying other materials such as glass the design possibilities are endless. Concrete is extremely durable, easy to clean and never needs to be replaced.

CONCRETE SLAB ICON SETS.

  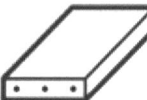 

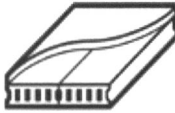 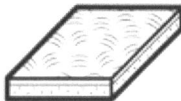 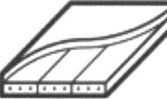 

 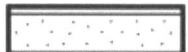 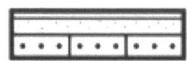 

6. Organic wool carpet

Carpet has long been a favorite go-to material for most homes. It is soft to walk on, comfortable to sit on and comes in a range of colors and patterns. Unfortunately, carpet has typically been made using volatile chemical compounds or toxins that are harmful to the environment and to our health. There are eco-friendly options though.

Consider carpets made of organic wool. Organic wool is a natural resource spun into a thread that can be dyed any color imaginable, and then be woven to create a carpet. It is one of the first materials to be used as a floor covering, is very durable and can last centuries. In some families wool rugs have been passed down from generation to generation making them family heirlooms. At the end of its useful life, the pile from wool carpet can be returned to the ground, where the nutrients released as it decomposes promote further grass growth, and the natural production cycle starts all over again. Under the right conditions, wool is totally biodegradable.

7. Corn Carpet

One of the newest environmentally fibers, Carpet is made of corn sugar. It is a very high performing carpet fiber. It is one of the best in terms of durability and the best in terms of stain resistance (in our opinion). Since utilizing corn sugar may take away from the animal and human feed, this may make it not as environmentally friendly as the previous two options. However, you could argue that the durability of Sorona Smartstrand makes it more eco-friendly than PET polyester. It depends on how you look at it. This is a very exciting new carpet fiber.

Corn carpets are made of 35% renewable materials. What are "renewable materials"? It typically refers to a plant because they can be re-grown. In this case, corn sugar is the renewable component. These carpets are made from propanediol, or Bio-PDO, a corn-based polymer. It is made from corn sugar, a by-product of making ethanol, generated at a nearby plant.

An E. coli bacteria --genetically-modified by DuPont scientists--breaks down the corn sugar through a fermentation process that is much like making beer.

DIY
How to make homemade natural wall coating from recycled clothes and fabrics

There are many reasons to use natural wall coating on your walls; like it being odor-free, sound insulation, moisture insulation, heat and cold insulation, crack resistant and quick and easy applicability. This natural coating can cover glass, ceramic, cement, brick, wood. It also has color diversity, acoustic insulation, high resistance against humidity, applicable on any surface, odore free, repairable, 100 % natural, clean environment, thermal Insulation, fire resistance, no more insect, light and many other benefits.

Recipes for homemade natural wall coating:
If you're wanting to ditch those toxic, commercial chemical paints for coating walls and switch to a more natural, homemade wall coating: this simple recipe will have you coating green in no time. However, before we get to the wall coating, let's check out some of the most common (and most useful) non-toxic products:

Small Shredder
Firstly, you need to purchase a $50 DIY shredder to crush recycling (if your paper shredder is strong enough for fabrics and used clothes, you can use it). It will be around $50 only if you have access to a waterjet cutter, but you most likely don't and the minimum will round to about $150. You can have your home shredder for textile, plastic and metal.

DIY: Steps for making homemade Eco friendly wall coating with used clothes and fabrics

Necessary items for start wall coating

- Recycled Fabrics and clothes
- Small home Yelca Shredder
- Added to Yelca powder and required water
- A plastic pan or basin in which shredded clothes, Yelca powder and water can be mixed.
- A medium or large size Yelca trowel or plastic trowel for rubbing and smoothing Yelca paste on the desired surface.

How to prepare Yelca dough:

Do the following steps in order and carefully:

Step 1: Collect used fabrics and clothes for as much that is needed

Step 2: Give it to the small home Yelca Shredder and start to shredding above mentioned fabrics and clothes

Step 3: Add required amount of Yelca powder

Step 4: Make and mix right amount of water with items mentioned in Step 1 and 2 in the existing plastic pan.

Step 5: After 15-30 minutes the dough is ready to be installed on the desired surface.

Step 6: The correct way to rub Yelca on the desired surface is to: first, thoroughly clean the surface of the wall to remove soot, dust or any obstacles to the adhesion of Yelca paste. Then, with a special Yelca trowel, spread the Yelca dough on the surface until it reaches a thickness of about one millimeter.

Step 7: Be careful in doing this and do not give up quickly because you may not be able to do it well the first time, however, with practice and repetition you can achieve a skill that covers both the entire surface with the dough and the thickness of the dough is minimal (not more than 0.5 mm to 1.5 mm).

Note: We've done our absolute best to provide the best information possible, but since we haven't tried every single one of these DIY items in every possible situation, we can't vouch for them 100 percent. So please be cautious and take many safety pre-cautions.

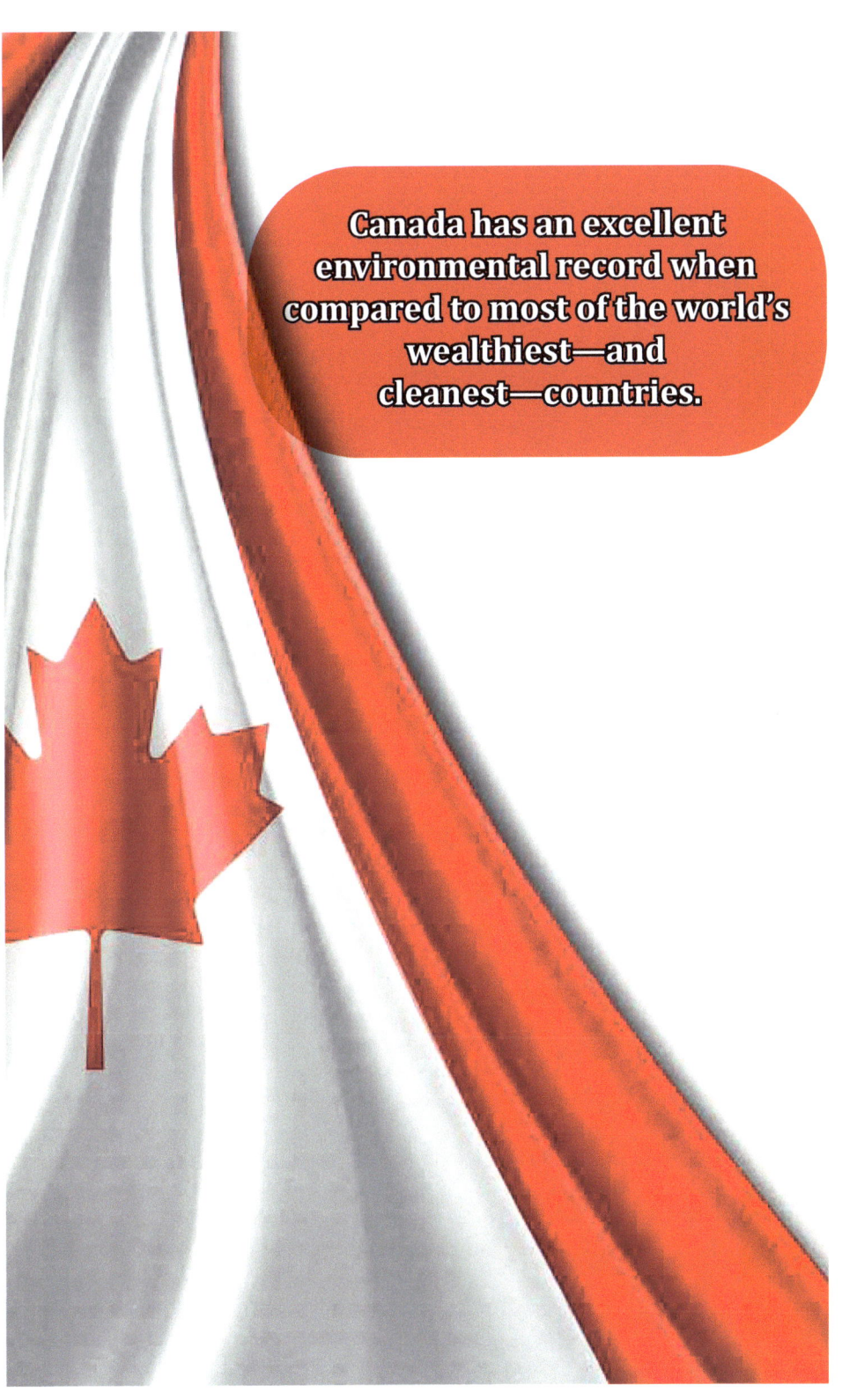

Canada has an excellent environmental record when compared to most of the world's wealthiest—and cleanest—countries.

1) We can create wall coating with used clothes and fabrics.
A) True
B) False
ANSWER:

2) You can have your _____ _____ for textile, plastic and metal.
A) home shredder
B) personal bag
C) plastic bag
D) water dispenser
ANSWER:

3) VOC is short for volatile organic compounds which produce harmful molecules.
A) True
B) False
ANSWER:

4) Eco-Friendly Ways to Renovate Your Home:
A) Use recycled glass
B) Use formaldehyde-free cabinets
C) Paint with low-VOC or VOC-free paint
D) Go solar
E) All of them
ANSWER:

5) Carpet has long been a favorite go-to material for most homes. It is soft to walk on, comfortable to sit on and comes in a range of colors and patterns.
A) True
B) False
ANSWER:

6) One of the newest environmentally fibers, Carpet is made of corn sugar. It is a very high performing carpet fiber. It is one of the best in terms of durability and the best in terms of stain resistance (in our opinion).
A) True
B) False
ANSWER:

7) Habitat for Humanity is one such retailer, but there are many across the country, some even specialize in high-end products. This can be a great and cost-effective way to redo your home.
A) True
B) False
ANSWER:

8) Describe ‹Vinyl›, is a synthetic made of chlorinated petrochemicals that are harmful.
A) True
B) False
ANSWER:

9) Re-face instead of replacing, As I just mentioned, the greatest expense of any kitchen remodel may very well be your cabinets. Instead of replacing them altogether, consider repainting them or simply refacing them.
A) True
B) False
ANSWER:

10) Using VOC-free products like paint will help you breathe easier when at home.
A) True
B) False
ANSWER:

11) _____ is commonly used in building materials and household products.
A) Formaldehyde
B) Propylene Glycol
C) Many Chemicals
D) Nicotine
ANSWER:

12) There are now many stores that offer _____ and formaldehyde-free furniture such.
A) VOC
B) BOD
C) FSC
D) Nano
ANSWER:

13) Linoleum is not new to the market; it fell out of favor with the introduction of _____ in the 1940's.
A) VOC
B) Vinyl
C) FSC
D) Nano
ANSWER:

14) What is a natural source of organic wool? Woven to create a carpet.
A) True
B) False
ANSWER:

15) What is a great way to start your morning? Natural lighting and morning sunshine.
A) True
B) False
ANSWER:

16) What is DIY? do it yourself
A) True
B) False
ANSWER:

17) Cork flooring is a product made from the bark of the cork oak tree, a material which is ground, processed into sheets and baked in a kiln to produce tiles that serve as flooring for offices, light commercial locations, and residences.
A) True
B) False
ANSWER:

18) Bamboo flooring is another wood like option that is gaining in popularity. It is actually a grass that shares similar characteristics as hardwood. It is durable, easy to maintain and is easy to install.
A) True
B) False
ANSWER:

19) Linoleum is one of the most natural and sustainable flooring solutions on the market, appreciated for its natural beauty, comfort and durability for over 150 years.
A) True
B) False
ANSWER:

20) Glass has similar benefits of other eco-friendly materials. It is non-absorptive and won't mildew or mold in damp environments. It is easy to maintain and won't stain
A) True
B) False
ANSWER:

21) Polished concrete is an unlikely sustainable material that is gaining in popularity. Concrete is typically slab on grade and used as a sub flooring in some residential settings.
A) True
B) False
ANSWER:

22) The greatest expense o of any kitchen remodel may very well be your cabinets. Instead of replacing them altogether, consider repainting them or simply refacing them. Most likely your cabinets are in great conditions. New doors and drawers can give seemingly tired cabinets a whole new life!
A) True
B) False
ANSWER:

Bibliography:

Amberg, N.; Magda, R. Environmental Pollution and Sustainability or the Impact of the Environmentally Conscious Measures of International Cosmetic Companies on Purchasing Organic Cosmetics. Visegrad J. Bioecon. Sustain. Dev. 2018, 1, 23.

Asadi, J., "International Environmental Labelling, Economic Consequencies, Export Magazine, July 2001

Asadi, J. 2008. Mobile Phone as management systems tools, ISO Magazine, Vol.8, No.1

Asadi, J., Eco-Labelling Standards, National Standard Magazine, Sep. 2004.

Balló, Z. Review of the competition between diy store review of the competition between diy store chains in Hungary. Delhi Bus. Rev. 2010, 11, 13–28.

Barbieux, D.; Padula, A.D. Paths and Challenges of New Technologies: The Case of Nanotechnology-Based Cosmetics Development in Brazil. Adm. Sci. 2018, 8, 16.

Basketter, D.; Corsini, E. Can We Make Cosmetic Contact Allergy History? Cosmetics 2016, 3, 11.

Bennett, A.; Guerra, P. DIY Cultures and Underground Music Scenes. Abingdon, Oxon; Routledge: New York, NY, USA, 2019; p. 315.

Benitta Christy P & Dr. Kavitha S, "GO-GREEN TEXTILES FOR ENVIRONMENT", Advanced Engineering and Applied Sciences: An International Journal 2014; 4(3): 26-28

Chemical Week, 1999. Europe's Beef Ban Tests Precautionary Principle. (August 11).

Chaudri, S.K.; Jain, N.K. History of Cosmetics. Asian J. Pharm. 2009, 7–9, 164–167.

CHOI, J.P. Brand Extension as Informational Leverage. Review of Eco- nomic Studies, Vol. 65 (1998), pp. 655-669.

Conway, G. 2000. Genetically modified crops: risks and promise.

Corrado, M., (1989), The Greening Consumer in Britain, MORI, London

Corrado, M., (1997), Green Behaviour – Sustainable Trends, Sustainable Lives?, MORI, london, accessed via countries. Manila, Asian Development Bank 33p.

Cosmetics, Perfume, & Hygiene in Ancient Egypt. Available online: https://www.ancient.eu/article/1061/cosmetics-perfume--hygiene-in-ancient-egypt/ (accessed on 4 May 2017).

Davies, Clive. Chief, Design for the Environment Program, Environmental Protection Agency. Interview. March 24, 2009.

Emilien, G.; Weitkunat, R.; Lüdicke, F. Consumer Perception of Product Risks and Benefits; Springer:

Berlin/Heidelberg, Germany, 2017; p. 596.

Fox, R.W.; Lears Jackson, T.J. The Culture of Consumption: Critical Essays in American History, 1880–1980; Pantheon Books: New York, NY, USA, 1983; p. 236.

Federal Trade Commission, "Sorting Out Green Advertising Claims." http://www.ftc. gov/bcp/edu/pubs/consumer/general/gen02.shtm (March 26, 2009, March 27, 2009)

MSNBC, "Do You Know What's in Your Cleaning Products?" http://today.msnbc.msn. com/id/29663739/ (March 17, 2009)

Ooyen, Carla. Research Manager with Nutrition Business Journal. Personal correspondence. March 19, 2009.

Tekin, Jenn. Marketing Manager with Packaged Facts & SBI. Personal correspondence. March 17, 2009.

University of California - Berkeley. http://berkeley.edu/news/media/releases/2006/05/22_ householdchemicals.shtml (March 26, 2009)

U.S. Department of Health and Human Services, Household Products Database.http:// householdproducts.nlm.nih.gov/cgi-bin/household/prodtree?prodcat=Inside+the+Home (March 17,

Women's Voices of the Earth, "Household Cleaning Products and Effects on Human Health."http://www.womenandenvironment.org/campaignsandprograms/SafeCleaning/ safecleaninghealth (March 17, 2009)

EMONS, W. Credence Goods Monopolists. International Journal of In- dustrial Organization, Vol. 19 (2001), pp. 375-389.

European Union official website: https://ec.europa.eu/info/about-european-commission/ contact_en

Feenstra, R.C. "Exact Hedonic Price Indexes," Review of Economics and Statistics 77 (1995): 634-653.

Feenstra, R.C., and J.A. Levinsohn. "Estimating Markups and Market Conduct with Multidimensional Product Attributes," Review of Economic Studies (62 (1995): 19-52.

Forest Stewardship Council: "Principles and criteria for forest stewardship" Document 1.2: <http://www.fscoax.org>

Forsyth, K. 1999. Will consumers pay more for certified wood products? Journal of Forestry 97 (2) : 18-22.

Freeman, A. M III. The Measurement of Environmental and Resource Values. Theory and Methods. Washington D.C.: Resource for the Future, 1993.

Friends of the Earth, 1993. Timber certification and eco-labeling. London, FOE:

Geetha Margret Soundri, "Ecofriendly Antimicrobial Finishing of Textiles Using Natural Extract", Journal of International Academic Research For Multidisciplinary, ISSN: 2320 – 5083, 2014, Vol 2.

Graves, P., J.C. Murdoch, M.A. Thayer, and D. Waldman. "The Robustness of Hedonic Price Estimation: Urban Air Quality," Land Economics 64(1988): 220-233.

Halvorsen, R. and R. Palmquist. "The Interpretation of Dummy Variables in Semilogarithmic Equations." American Economic Review 70:474-75 (1980).

Imhoff, Dan, and Grose, Lynda, and Carra, Roberto., "Organic Cotton Exhibit," Mimeo. Simple Life and distributed the Texas Organic Cotton Marketing Cooperative, O'Donnell, Texas (1996).

Imhoff, Dan. "Growing Pains: Organic Cotton Tests the Fibre of Growers and Manufacturers Alike," reprinted on Simple Life's web page (simplelife.com), but first printed by Farmer to Farmer, December 1995.

Incomplete Consumer Information in Laboratory Markets. Journal of Environmental labeling.

ISO 14020, ISO 14021,ISO 14024,ISO 14025, International Organization for Standardization.

Kennedy, P.E. "Estimation with Correctly Interpreted Dummy Variables in Semilogarithmic Equations," American Economic Review 71: 801 (1981).

Kirchho®, S., (2000), Green Business and Blue Angels.

Kraus, Jeff. Lab Technician at the North Carolina School of Textiles.

Labeling Issues, Policies and Practices Worldwide.

Lamport, L. 1998. The cast of (timber) certifiers: who are they? International J. Ecoforestry 11(4): 118-122.

Large Scale impoverishment of Amazonian forests by logging and fire. 1999.

Lathrop, K.W. and Centner, T.J. 1998. Eco-labeling and ISO 14000: An analysis of US regulatory systems and issues concerning adoption of type II standards. Environmental

Lee, J. et al. 1996. Trade related environmental measures; sizing and comparing impacts.

Lehtonen, Markku. 1997. Criteria in Environmental Labeling: A comparative Analysis on Environmental Criteria in Selected Labeling Schemes. Geneva, UNEP. 148p.

LIEBI, T. Trusting Labels: A Matter of Numbers? Working Paper Uni versity of Bern, No. 0201 (2002).

Lindstrom, T. 1999. Forest Certification: The View from Europe's NIPFs. Journal of Forestry 97(3): 25-31. London

Losey, J.E., Rayor, L.S. & Carter, M.E. 1999. Transgenic pollen harms monarch larvae. Nature 399 20 May): p.214.

Management 22 (2) : 163-172.

Mattoo, A. and H. V. Singh, (1994), Eco-Labelling: Policy Considera-Michaels, R. G., and V. K. Smith. "Market Segmentation And Valuing Amenities With Hedonic Models: The Case Of Hazardous Waste Sites," Journal of Urban Economics, 1990 28(2), 223-242.

Nicholson-Lord, D., (1993) 'Tis the Season to be Green, The Independent, 20 December Nuttall, N., (1993), Shoppers can cross green products off their lists, The Times, 3 July OCDE/GD(97)105. Paris, OECD. 81p.

OECD. "Ec-labelling: Actual Effects of Selected Programmes," OCDE/GD (97) 105, 1997, Paris. (available on line at http://www.oecd.org/env/eco/books.htm#trademono)

OECD. 1997a. Case study on eco-labeling schemes. Paris, OECD (30 Dec):

OECD. 1997b. Eco-labeling: Actual Effects of Selected Programs.

Osborne, L. "Market Structure, Hedonic Models, and the Valuation of Environmental Amenities." Unpublished Ph.D. dissertation. North Carolina State University, 1995.

Osborne, L., and V. K. Smith. "Environmental Amenities, Product Differentiation, and market Power," Mimeo, 1997.

Ozanne, L.K. and Vlosky, R.P. 1996. Wood products environmental certification: the United States perspective". Forestry Chronicle 72 (2) : 157-165.

Palmquist, R. B., F. M. Roka, and T.Vukina. "Hog Operations, Environmental Effects, and Residential Property Values," Land Economics 73(1), (1997): 114-24.

Palmquist, R.B. "Hedonic Methods," in J.B Braden and C.D. Kolstad, eds. Measuring the Demand for Environmental Improvement. Amsterdam, NL: Elsevier, 1991.

Pento, T. 1997. Implementation of Public Green Procurement Programs (22-31) in Greener Purchasing: Opportunities and Innovations. Sheffield, Greenleaf Publ. 325 p.

Perloff, J. "Industrial Organization Lecture Notes," Mimeo. University of California at Berkeley (1985).

Plant, C. and Plant, J. 1991. Green business: hope or hoax? Philadelphia, New Society Publishers 136 p.

Polak, J. and Bergholm, K. 1997. Eco-labeling and trade: a cooperative approach (Jan.): Policy in a Green Market. Environmental and Resource Economics 22, 419-

Poore, M.E.D. et al. 1989. No timber without trees. London, Earthscan. 352p.

Raff, D. M.G., and M. Trajtenberg. "Quality-Adjusted Prices for the American Automobile Industry: 1906-1940." NBER Working Paper Series, Working Paper No. 5035, February 1995.

Roberts, J. T. 1998. Emerging global environment standards: prospects and perils. Journal of Developing Societies 14 (1): 144-163.

Rosen, S., "Hedonic Prices and Implicit Markets: Product Differentiation in Pure Competition." Journal of Political Economy. 82: 34-55 (1974).

Ross, B. 1997. Eco-friendly procurement training course for UN HCR. : 126 p.

Ryan, S., and Skipworth, M., (1993), Consumers turn their backs on green revolution, The Times, 4 April

Salzman, J. 1997. Informing the Green Consumer: The Debate over the Use and Abuse of Environmental Labels. Journal of Industrial Ecology 1 (2): 11-22.

Sanders, W. 1997. Environmentally Preferable Purchasing: The US Experience (946-960) in Greener Purchasing: Opportunities and Innovations. Sheffield, Greenleaf Publ. 325p.

Sayre, D. 1996. Inside ISO 14000: The competitive advantage of environmental management. Delray Beach FL., St. Lucie Press. 232p.

SHAPIRO, C. Premiums for High Quality Products as Returns to Reputa- tion. Quarterly Journal of Economics, Vol. 98, No. 4 (1983), pp. 659-680.

Stillwell, M. and van Dyke, B. 1999. An activists handbook on genetically modified organisms and the WTO. Washington DC., The Consumer's Choice Council: 20 p.

Semenzato, A.; Costantini, A.; Meloni, M.; Maramaldi, G.; Meneghin, M.; Baratto, G. Formulating O/W Emulsions with Plant-Based Actives: A Stability Challenge for an Eective Product. Cosmetics 2018, 5, 59.

Teisl, M. F., B. Roe, and R. L. Hicks. "Can Eco-labels tune a market? Evidence from dolphin-safe labeling," Presented paper at the 1997 American Agricultural Economics Association Meetings, Toronto.

THE GERSEN, C. Psychological Determinants of Paying Attention to Eco- Labels in Purchase Decisions: Model Development and Multinational Vali- dation. Journal of Consumer Policy, Vol. 23, No. 4 (2000), pp. 285-313.

Tibor, T. and Feldman, I. 1995. ISO 14000: a guide to the new environmental management standards. Burr Ridge Ill., Irwin Professional Publ. 250 p.

Torre, I. de la, & Batker, D. K. (n.d.) 1999-2000. Prawn to trade: prawn to consume. Graham WA., Industrial Shrimp Action Network (isatorre@seanet.com), [and] Asia –Pacific

Townsend, M. 1998. Making things greener: motivations and influences in the greening of manufacturing. Aldershot, England, Ashgate Publisher. 203p.

U.S. Energy Information Administration, What is U.S. Electricity Generation by Energy Source?, Retrieved From: https://www.eia.gov/tools/faqs/faq.php?id=427&t=3

U.S. Energy Information Administration, Biomass Explained, Retrieved From: https://www.eia.gov/energyexplained/?page=biomass_home

U.S. Environmental Protection Agency. National Water Quality Fact Inventory: 1990 Report to Congress. EPA 503-9-92-006, Apr. 1992.

UK Eco-labelling Board website, accessed via http://www.ecosite.co.uk/Ecolabel-UK/

US Environmental Protection Agency (EPA742-R-99-001): 40 p. <www.epa.gov/opptintr/epp>

US EPA, 1993. Determinants of effectiveness for environmental certification and labeling programs. Washington, D.C., US Environmental Protect

US EPA, 1993. Status report on the use of environmental labels worldwide. Washington, D.C., US Environmental Protection Agency (742-R-93-001 September).

US EPA, 1993. The use of life-cycle assessment in environmental labeling. Washington, D.C., US Environmental Protection Agency (742-R-93-003 September).

US EPA, 1998. Environmental labeling: issues, policies, and practices worldwide. Washington DC., Environmental Protection Agency, Pollution Prevention Division Prepared by Abt

US EPA, 1999. Comprehensive procurement guidelines (CPG) program. Washington, D.C., US Environmental Protection Agency: <www.epa.gov/cpg>

US EPA, 1999. Environmentally preferable purchasing program: Private sector pioneers: How companies are incorporating environmentally preferable purchases. Washington, D.C.,

USG, 1993. Federal acquisition, recycling, and waste prevention. Washington DC., Executive Order: (20 October).

USG, 1998. Greening the government through waste prevention, recycling, and federal acquisition. Washington, D.C., Executive Order 13101 (September).

Kijjoa, A.; Sawangwong, P. Drugs and Cosmetics from the Sea. Mar. Drugs 2004, 2, 73–82. [CrossRef]

Wang, J.; Pan, L.; Wu, S.; Lu, L.; Xu, Y.; Zhu, Y.; Guo, M.; Zhuang, S. Recent Advances on Endocrine Disrupting Eects of UV Filters. Int. J. Environ. Res. Public Health 2016, 13, 782.

Bilal, A.I.; Tilahun, Z.; Shimels, T.; Gelan, Y.B.; Osman, E.D. Cosmetics Utilization Practice in Jigjiga Town, Eastern Ethiopia: A Community Based Cross-Sectional Study. Cosmetics 2016, 3, 40.

Ting, C.T.; Hsieh, C.M.; Chang, H.-P.; Chen, H.-S. Environmental Consciousness and Green Customer Behavior: The Moderating Roles of Incentive Mechanisms. Sustainability 2019, 11, 819.

Chen, K.; Deng, T. Research on the Green Purchase Intentions from the Perspective of Product Knowledge. Sustainability 2016, 8, 943.

Wang, H.; Ma, B.; Bai, R. How Does Green Product Knowledge Eectively Promote Green Purchase Intention? Sustainability 2019, 11, 1193.

Wolf, M.; McQuitty, S. Understanding the Do-it-Yourself Consumer: DIY Motivations and Outcomes. Acad. Mark. Sci. Rev. 2013, 1, 154–170.

Mintel. DIY Review 2005; Mintel: London, UK, 2005.

Miller, D. Material Culture and Mass Consumption; Blackwell: Oxford, UK, 1987; p. 252.

Nguyen, T.T.H.; Yang, Z.; Nguyen, N.; Johnson, L.W.; Cao, T.K. Greenwash and Green Purchase Intention: The Mediating Role of Green Skepticism. Sustainability 2019, 11, 2653.

Cinelli, P.; Coltelli, M.B.; Signori, F.; Morganti, P.; Lazzeri, A. Cosmetic Packaging to Save the Environment: Future Perspectives. Cosmetics 2019, 6, 26.

Eixarch, H.; Wyness, L.; Siband, M. The Regulation of Personalized Cosmetics in the EU. Cosmetics 2019, 6, 29.

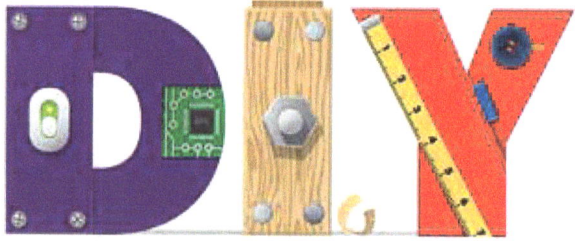

CANADA SILVER BEAVER BADGE

Participate in our Online Classes to earn these exclusive digital badges!
www.toptenaward.org

Design & Development by:

Tara Asadi

CANADA BRONZE BEAVER BADGE

Participate in our Online Classes to earn these exclusive digital badges!
www.toptenaward.org

Design & Development by:

Tara Asadi

CANADA GOLD BEAVER BADGE

Participate in our Online Classes to earn these exclusive digital badges!

Design & Development by:

Tara Asadi

Environmental Lifestyle Guide

For Grade 9

For Grade 10

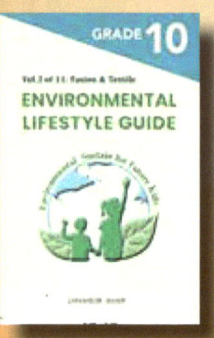  

Plus Online Certification Tests via:
https://toptenaward.org

Standard Text Books

For Grade 11

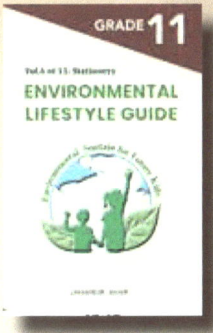  

For Grade 12

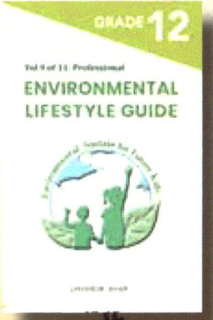 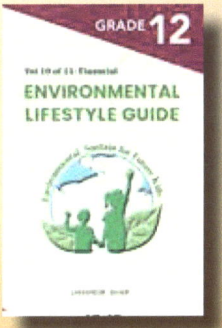 

**Environmental Lifestyle Guide
Standard Text Book**
For Students Grade 9 to 12
Available in more than
39,000 Bookstores
all over the globe.
https://ecofriendlyeducation.com

Cooperation by:
Top Ten Award International Network
&
Environmental Sustain for Future Kids

www.ingramcontent.com/pod-product-compliance
Lightning Source LLC
Chambersburg PA
CBHW040858120626
46551CB00001B/78